Transpose

vt.

to change in form or nature : transform

to render into another language, style, or manner of expression : translate

to transfer from one place or period to another : shift

to change the relative place or normal order of : alter the sequence of

to write or perform (a musical composition) in a different key

to bring (a term) from one side of an algebraic equation to the other with change of sign.

TRANSPOSES

BY DYLAN EDWARDS

Book design by Charles "Zan" Christensen

Edwards, Dylan
Transposes
ISBN-13: 978-0-9845940-8-5
ISBN-10: 0-9845940-8-6

First Northwest Press edition, September 2012.

Printed in Canada

Contents

Author's Note

The stories you are about to read are all true accounts from interviews I conducted with the principal characters. They have been dramatized for comics, and as such, some minor characters may be composites, and some framing devices invented (Henry does not, for example, work as a doyen in a museum dedicated exclusively to the minutiae of his life).

All primary participants and secondary characters have been given pseudonyms to protect their privacy, and some identifying information has been altered. Also, the character designs are not intended to be accurate representations of the individuals in real life (that privacy thing, again).

Foreword

Dylan Edwards is not just a good cartoonist, he's apparently also a very good listener. In this book, he has undertaken the delicate task of turning other peoples' real life experiences, in all their intimate complexity, into stories for public consumption. His subjects—seven different queer-identified transmen—have entrusted him, in a sense, with their lives.

That trust is well deserved. Edwards handles the material he has been given with respect, empathy, humor, and impeccable line work. This would probably be enough. But add manifest love to the mix, and something sublime starts to happen. Edwards clearly loves these guys, and we come to love them too.

As he says in his introduction, "You might be tempted to think that 'queer-identified female-to-male transperson' is such a narrowly defined subset of a subset (of a subset!) that surely their stories can't be all that varied."

But the stories he proceeds to tell are radiantly diverse and richly particular, beginning with Cal's. There's no confusion or struggle here, just a confident guy coping resourcefully with an awkward situation. Next, Henry loves to categorize things, but eludes any tidy categorization himself. He embraces "transition as a state of being rather than a temporary phase."

Adam is in a lesbian relationship with a girlfriend who pushes him to explore his "gender stuff" in therapy. Their breakup, when Adam finally comes out as trans, is bittersweet. Blake shows us the particular challenges a trans person with an STI faces in dealing with the medical establishment. Avery lives with his non-gendered ex, hooks up with genderqueer guys, hooks up with genderqueer guys, and is in a 24/7 relationship with his dissertation.

The intertwined stories of Aaron and James are especially resonant. In this masterpiece, Edwards uses inventive graphic technique to show two complex lives gradually converging. As the protagonists struggle to attain some kind of congruence within their own selves, they move closer and closer to an intersection with each other.

I love the page where James looks hungrily at Aaron's hairline and beard stubble and the outline of his deltoid muscle and realizes that he wants to look like that too.

The medium of comics is perhaps especially appropriate for stories about people for whom appearance is such a pivotal issue. It's really kind of staggering how many degrees and styles of masculinity Edwards limns in these pages.

Comics also solves an interesting problem inherent to the trans experience. Language can be confusing when discussing someone's pre-transition past. But that problem recedes when the storytelling is primarily visual. In flashbacks to some of the characters' childhoods, we see them as female-bodied children, but there's no need to encumber them with pronouns. Somehow this freedom from language allows to also see these kids, seamlessly, as the men they will eventually become.

Seeing ourselves reflected accurately in the world is crucial to a sense of well-being, to feeling whole and real. The reflections of queer FTM experience that Edwards gives us here are sharply focused, delicately nuanced, and shot through with a warm humanity. He has created, he tells us, the book that he always wished he could have had himself.

But he has also created a gift for everyone else. Especially if you've never had to wonder about who you are or who you want, or what, if anything, those things might have to do with one another, *Transposes* will teach you something about what it means to have a body and to feel desire. About what it means, in short, to be human.

Alison Bechdel
August, 2012

WAIT, I HAVE TO GIVE A SPEECH?!

I... I CAN'T... I...

...LEFT MY REGULAR GLASSES IN THE CAR!

I CAN'T GO OUT THERE IN PRESCRIPTION SUNGLASSES.

I'LL LOOK LIKE AN ASS.

AHEM. YOU MAKE A PERSUASIVE ARGUMENT.

SKREEK SKREEK

EH. SO. HI!

YOU, UH, PROBABLY WANT TO KNOW WHAT THIS BOOK IS ABOUT AND WHY I WROTE IT.

WELL, TO PUT IT OVERLY CLINICALLY, IT'S ABOUT QUEER-IDENTIFIED FEMALE-TO-MALE TRANSPEOPLE, OR QFTMS.

THIS BOOK FEATURES REAL PEOPLE'S STORIES ABOUT THEIR EXPERIENCES AS QFTMS. I INTERVIEWED THEM, AND TURNED LITTLE BITS OF THEIR LIVES INTO COMICS.

TAKKA TAKKA

YOU MIGHT BE TEMPTED TO THINK THAT "QUEER-IDENTIFIED FEMALE-TO-MALE TRANSPERSON" IS SUCH A NARROWLY DEFINED SUBSET OF A SUBSET (OF A SUBSET!) THAT SURELY THEIR STORIES CAN'T BE ALL THAT VARIED.

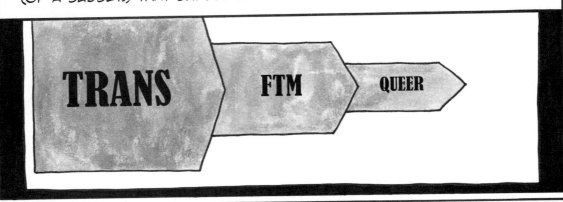

TRANS → FTM → QUEER

AND YET, VARIED THEY ARE. FROM GENDERQUEERS TO STAUNCHLY MALE-IDENTIFIED GAY GUYS, TO TRANSMEN WHO DATE OTHER TRANSMEN.

ADAM   HENRY   CAL   AVERY

BLAKE   AARON   JAMES

FROM VANILLA TO KINKY, MONOGAMOUS TO POLY, EACH PERSON'S STORY IS A UNIQUE TAKE ON THE QFTM IDENTITY.

4

IT'S ABOUT CAL, HENRY, ADAM, BLAKE, AVERY, AARON, AND JAMES.

IN OTHER WORDS, THESE ARE STORIES ABOUT INDIVIDUALS WHO, VIA THE MEDIUM OF THEIR LIVES, CREATE THEIR OWN INTERPRETATIONS OF WHAT IT MEANS TO BE A QUEER-IDENTIFIED FEMALE-TO-MALE TRANSPERSON.

THE END RESULT IS THE BOOK I ALWAYS WANTED TO HAVE, MYSELF.

BUT ENOUGH YAMMERING FROM ME. I THINK IT'S TIME TO LET THESE GUYS TAKE THE STAGE.

CUE THE MUSIC, MAESTRO...

CAL

THEN I FIND OUT I'M GOING TO BE TOPPING A GENETIC GUY, AND ALL THE STUFF I NEEDED I LEFT AT HOME!

DID YOU MANAGE TO HIT UP THAT QUEER-FRIENDLY SEX SHOP I TOLD YOU ABOUT?

I DID! I HEADED OVER TO GLORIA'S HOLE LIKE YOU SUGGESTED...

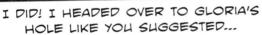

Christopher St Station
Downtown
① 1

GLORIA'S HOLE

EROTIC BOUTIQUE

I SHOULD BE A LOT MORE NERVOUS THAN I ACTUALLY AM. TOPPING A GUY. A GENETIC GUY! I'VE BEEN *WANTING* TO DO THIS, BUT...

I JUST THOUGHT I'D BE DOING IT WITH ANOTHER TRANSGUY FIRST.

AND FOR ME TO DO THAT WITHOUT HAVING HAD ANY SURGERY, BUT STILL FEEL LIKE HE WAS GETTING OFF ON MY MALENESS...

HENRY

MY BEST (AND ONLY) FRIEND WAS THE FUNDAMENTALIST PREACHER'S DAUGHTER. SHE TAUGHT ME ABOUT PROSTITUTION BY HAVING BROWN-HAIRED KEN PIMP OUT BARBIE AND MIDGE TO BLOND KEN.

A GROUP OF GIRLS DISCOVERED US HOLDING HANDS DURING RECESS ONE DAY.

LESBIANS!

I HAD NO IDEA WHAT THE WORD MEANT.

YEARS LATER, WHEN I WAS 12 OR SO, MY PARENTS BOUGHT ME A COPY OF *CHANGING BODIES, CHANGING LIVES*, AN EXCELLENT BOOK THAT DEFINED THE TERM.

OH, CRAP! IT'S TRUE!

AT THE TIME I ENDEAVOURED NOT TO THINK ABOUT IT.

...ESCENCE   TEENAGE YEARS

BUT BY THE TIME MY TEENAGE YEARS (AND HORMONES) WERE IN FULL SWING, I WAS QUITE POLITICIZED, WAITING TO COME OUT TO ALL AND SUNDRY.

SO I WENT OFF TO A WOMEN'S COLLEGE, DETERMINED TO MEET SOME REAL LESBIANS.

WHEREUPON I PROMPTLY FELL IN LOVE WITH A MAN.

C'EST LA VIE.

GENDER ROLEPLAY IN THE BEDROOM RIPPED THE LID OFF A NOTION I'D HARBOURED SINCE I WAS 14:

THAT I OUGHT TO BE IN A MALE BODY.

I WAS TRYING SO HARD TO CONTROL THESE ASPECTS OF MYSELF THAT THEY UNWOUND LIKE A MAINSPRING WHEN I LET THEM.

CUE LOTS OF CRYING IN MY FRIENDS' DORM ROOMS...

AWKWARDNESS WITH MY KIND BUT HOPELESSLY STRAIGHT BOYFRIEND...

AND READING THE ENORMOUSLY HELPFUL *TRANSGENDER WARRIORS.*

(I DO BEST IF I CAN PUT MYSELF IN HISTORICAL CONTEXT.)

LOOKING AT MY BEST MALE ROLE MODEL, MY FATHER, I DETERMINED THAT MACHISMO ISN'T ALL IT'S CRACKED UP TO BE.

ER, HE DID MASTERFUL CARVINGS OF OTHER THINGS AS WELL.

APPARENTLY IT HAD STARTED LIFE AS A PIECE OF FIREWOOD, THE SHAPE OF WHICH STRUCK HIM AS ENTERTAINING.

I REMEMBER SEEING HIM MAKING THIS PIECE, WHEN I WAS FAR TOO YOUNG TO UNDERSTAND WHAT IT WAS.

I WAS REACHING UP TO ADMIRE THE SMOOTHNESS OF THE FINISH.

WOULD YOU MIND NOT WORKING ON THAT THING WHILE THE KIDS ARE AROUND?!

I DIDN'T SEE THE PHALLUS TOTEM AGAIN UNTIL AFTER I HIT PUBERTY.

IT WAS SEQUESTERED ON A HIGH SHELF IN MY PARENTS' BEDROOM, A DOUBLY FORBIDDEN AREA.

SO OF COURSE I WENT RIGHT TO IT WHEN LEFT ALONE IN THE HOUSE.

IT WAS IN USE AS A BOOKEND, HOLDING UP, AMONG OTHER THINGS, A HARDBOUND COLLECTION OF ARTICLES FROM *SCREW*, THAT INCLUDED JUST *ONE* ARTICLE ON GAY SEX.

SCREW MAGAZINE 2600

COMPLICOPULATION

The Joy of Sects: A DOZEN DELIGHTFUL DENOMINATIONS

KARMA SUTURES

NAUGHTY POTTERY & ANCIENT GREECE DON'T WORRY, THIS TOTALLY COUNTS AS "ART"

AN ARTICLE I READ REPEATEDLY UNTIL THE BOOK FELL OPEN NATURALLY TO THAT PAGE.

LET'S JUST SAY THIS WAS NOT THE LAST ARTICLE ON GAY SEX I WAS TO ENJOY.

AY NU

G PORR V - Z

DOLL COLLECTIONS →

MEMORIA LIBRARY
• PRINT EDITIONS
FANFIC WING →

I'M FAR TOO FAGGY TO BE A "REAL MAN."

CHILDHOOD COLLECTION

OLLS

NOW I DON'T EVEN KNOW THAT I'M SO BENT ON BEING A "MAN."

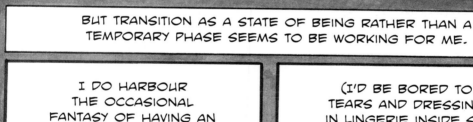

I DO SOMETIMES WISH MY BODY WERE MORE LIKE A GENETIC MAN'S, BUT SURGERY IS EXPENSIVE AND I HAVE OTHER PLANS FOR MY MONEY.

CHILDHOOD

I SUPPOSE IF I WERE MORE INTENT ON THIS...

ORIGINAL CREATIONS

...I'D FIND THE CASH SOMEHOW.

BUT TRANSITION AS A STATE OF BEING RATHER THAN A TEMPORARY PHASE SEEMS TO BE WORKING FOR ME.

I DO HARBOUR THE OCCASIONAL FANTASY OF HAVING AN UNCOMPLICATED GENDER.

(I'D BE BORED TO TEARS AND DRESSING IN LINGERIE INSIDE SIX HOURS, I KNOW.)

HONESTLY? BECAUSE THE AVENGERS HAVE THE BEST HAIRCUTS OF ANY OF THE LESBIANS I'VE MET SO FAR.

DOESN'T MAKE FOR GOOD TASTE IN MUSIC, UNFORTUNATELY. THAT'S WHY I WAS SO EXCITED ABOUT YOUR SMITHS SHIRT.

MEANT I COULD HIT ON YOU WITHOUT HAVING TO PRETEND TO LIKE THE INDIGO GIRLS.

HERE'S YOUR CHECK, SIR.

I BELIEVE YOU MEAN "MA'AM."

I'M SO SORRY! I --

NO, IT'S FINE.

DO YOU JUST WANT TO SPLIT IT DOWN THE MIDDLE, MARNI?

S-SURE.

41

42

43

SCRAMBLED, RIGHT? LOTS OF PEPPER?

AND YOU TAKE YOUR COFFEE BLACK WITH SUGAR?

HEY, I GOTTA SKIP THE AVENGERS MEETING THIS AFTERNOON. I HAVE AN APPOINTMENT WITH MY SHRINK.

MORE POWER TO YOU. I'VE NEVER HAD ANY LUCK WITH THERAPY.

NO?

I ALWAYS HAVE THE SAME DAMN CONVERSATION WITH EVERY THERAPIST I SEE. IT NEVER GETS ANYWHERE.

WHAT'S THE CONVERSATION?

45

I DIDN'T WANT TO COME RIGHT OUT AND SAY, "HEY, I THINK YOU MIGHT BE TRANS." SO WE'VE MOSTLY BEEN TALKING IN HYPOTHETICALS.

SHE'S THE DIRECTOR OF THE TRANS RESOURCE CENTER, AND MAY BE ABLE TO HELP POINT YOU IN THE RIGHT DIRECTION.

47

HIS STORY FOLLOWED AN "I ALWAYS KNEW I WAS A STRAIGHT GUY AND I ALWAYS KNEW I LIKED STRAIGHT WOMEN" TRAJECTORY.

SAME THING I KEEP READING OVER AND OVER.

ARE YOU FAMILIAR WITH LOU SULLIVAN?

NO.

HE WAS THE ONE WHO GOT THE MEDICAL ESTABLISHMENT TO ACKNOWLEDGE THAT GAY FTMS ACTUALLY EXIST.

HE LIVED FULL-TIME AS A GAY MAN.

WOW, THAT'S REALLY...

WOW.

GENDER STUFF GENDER STUFF GENDER STUFF GENDER STUFF GENDER ST...

STUFF GENDER STUFF GENDER STUFF GENDER STUFF GENDER STUFF...

STUFF GENDER STUFF GENDER STUFF GENDER STUFF GENDER...

GENDER STU...

DID YOU EVER CALL THAT THERAPIST JESSICA RECOMMENDED?

N-NOT YET. I WAS GOING TO... I'LL CALL HER AFTER THE HOLIDAYS.

THAT'S, LIKE, A MONTH FROM NOW.

YEAH, BUT SURELY SHE'S TOO BUSY TO SEE ME BEFORE THE NEW YEAR, SO...

SO MAKE AN APPOINTMENT ANYWAY.

GO INTO THE BEDROOM AND DON'T COME OUT UNTIL YOU'VE CALLED HER.

50

RING

RING RI- *click*

HELLO, DR. ATHANS' OFFICE.

UH. H-HI. I THINK, UH, I MIGHT BE AN FTM? SO, UH, I WAS CALLING TO MAKE AN APPOINTMENT?

I ALSO HAVE A SPOT FIRST THING WEDNESDAY, IF THAT'S BETTER.

OKAY, WOULD TUESDAY AT 2:00 WORK FOR YOU?

N-NO, TUESDAY'S FINE. SEE YOU THEN.

AH! TH-THAT'S IN THREE DAYS.

GENDER STUFF?

GENDER STUFF.

GENDER STUFF.

GENDER STUFF.

GENDER STUFF!

GENDER STUFF.

HEY! HOW WAS THERAPY?

WOW, IT WAS GREAT! ALL THIS STUFF IS COMING OUT. MY WHOLE LIFE IS SUDDENLY STARTING TO MAKE SENSE!

I *LOVE* IT WHEN PEOPLE CALL ME "ADAM" AND "HE"! I NEVER WANT TO HEAR MY BIRTH NAME OR FEMALE PRONOUNS AGAIN!

I'M PASSING AS MALE ABOUT 90 PERCENT OF THE TIME. AND THAT'S WITHOUT *T*!

OOH! OOH! I STOPPED BY THE THRIFT STORE ON THE WAY HOME AND THE CUTE GAY GUY WAS THERE!

THANK YOU, SIR, AND HAVE A *FABULOUS* DAY!

THANK *YOU!*

I THINK HE MAY ACTUALLY HAVE BEEN FLIRTING WITH ME!

HOW COOL!

I THINK IT'S GREAT YOU'RE FINALLY GETTING ALL THIS FIGURED OUT.

BUT.

SHHHHH

BUT?

BUT.

LOOK.

ADAM.

I AM VERY, VERY PROUD OF YOU FOR DOING WHAT IS SO OBVIOUSLY THE RIGHT THING FOR YOU.

BUT I'M A LESBIAN.

I NEED TO BE WITH A WOMAN, AND THAT'S NOT GOING TO HAPPEN WITH YOU.

I'M SORRY. DO YOU UNDERSTAND WHY WE NEED TO BREAK UP?

THE FIRST THING I THOUGHT WHEN I LOOKED AT MYSELF IN THE MIRROR, DRESSED IN A JACKET AND TIE FOR THE CHRISTMAS PARTY, WAS...

"THIS IS GOING COMPLETELY AGAINST MARNI'S IDENTITY."

I GUESS IT WAS KIND OF A FLUKE THAT WE GOT TOGETHER IN THE FIRST PLACE.

TRUTH IS, I DON'T THINK I COULD BE CAMP ENOUGH FOR YOU ANYWAY.

HA!

BLAKE

NICE CHEST!

THANKS!

HE MUST'VE HAD KEYHOLE. WONDER WHO HIS SURGEON WAS?

I HAVE SOMETHING TO SHOW YOU THAT I THINK YOU'LL APPRECIATE.

I'LL BET YOU DO.

CHECK OUT MY APPENDECTOMY SCAR!

SO! WHAT DO YOU LIKE TO DO?

UH, WHOA.

DON, LISTEN.

LISTENING!

BEFORE WE GO ANY FURTHER. I'M A TRANSGUY. THE SCARS ON MY CHEST ARE FROM MY TOP SURGERY.

WELL, I STILL THINK YOU'RE HOT. I'VE NEVER BEEN WITH A TRANSGUY BEFORE!

IN THAT CASE, LET ME GET MY TOOLS!

I JUST WANTED TO MAKE SURE THIS IS GONNA BE SAFE FOR ME TO USE... UH...

YOU KNOW...

DOWN THERE.

YOU DON'T NEED THAT.

O-KAAAY. THANKS.

SHOVE!

HEY, I'M NOT GONNA MAKE IT IN TO WORK TODAY.

NOPE, NOT REALLY FEELING ANY BETTER.

YEAH, GOT AN APPOINTMENT THIS AFTERNOON. I'LL LET YOU KNOW WHAT'S UP.

I CAN'T TAKE THIS WAITING. WHAT IF I *DO* HAVE AN STI?

FIRST TIME FOR EVERYTHING?

IT WAS JUST SO DAMN HOT, NOT BEING ALL ANGSTY ABOUT THE TRANS THING FOR ONCE.

A LITTLE *TOO* HOT, I GUESS.

NOW I'M GONNA HAVE *ANOTHER* BIG, COMPLICATED THING TO COME OUT ABOUT.

EH, I WOULDN'T BOTHER. NO ONE HAS EVER, EVEN ONCE, DISCLOSED TO ME THAT HE HAD AN STI.

COME ON, JASON. THAT'S JUST –

RING

HELLO?

SPEAKING.

HERPES
SIMPLEX
VIRUS.

MY BOYFRIEND AND I... UH... AND
CONDOMS... NOT SO MUCH.
SO... YEAH.

SKITCH
SKITCH

BOYFRIEND??

BOYFRIEND.

OPEN

CAKESPLOSION

69

AVERY

WELL? WHAT DID YOU THINK?

IT WAS REALLY GOOD!

HAD YOU EVER HAD SCALLOPS BEFORE?

I'D NEVER EVEN *HEARD* OF SCALLOPS BEFORE!

AT THE TIME, I DIDN'T KNOW HE WAS DYING.

BUT I HAVE VERY DISTINCT MEMORIES OF THAT DAY.

I DON'T GUESS YOUR DAD WOULD BE TOO HAPPY TO SEE ALL THAT FROU-FROU FOOD!

HE WOULD SAY, "WHAT IS *THAT?*"

THEN HE'D SAY, "GIMME SOME REAL FOOD. GIMME SOME CHICKEN-FRIED STEAK!

SOUNDS LIKE... TUCKER.

WELL! DISHES ARE ALL DONE. YOU READY TO HEAD TO THE PLANETARIUM?

AREN'T WE GOING TO GET IN THE CAR?

I NOW REALIZE HE PLANNED THIS DAY VERY CAREFULLY.

TONY'S CAFÉ

YOU'RE NOT IN THE SUBURBS ANYMORE, DOROTHY!

THE PLANETARIUM IS JUST A COUPLE BLOCKS DOWN THIS WAY. IT'S FASTER TO WALK THAN IT IS TO DRIVE.

HERSTO BOOK

THIS IS HOW HE WANTED TO BE REMEMBERED.

BY THE TIME I WAS APPLYING FOR COLLEGE I KNEW I WAS QUEER, AND I NEEDED SOMEWHERE SAFE TO COME OUT. THE PUBLIC REASON I GAVE FOR MY CHOICE OF UNIVERSITY, WHILE ACCURATE, WAS A BIT SELECTIVE.

BECAUSE WOMEN'S COLLEGES HAVE MUCH BETTER PLACEMENT RECORDS FOR WOMEN IN THE SCIENCES THAN CO-ED SCHOOLS DO.

WHAT THE HELL IS *THIS?*

YOU DON'T NEED GOOD *PLACEMENT.* WHAT YOU *NEED* IS A GOOD HUSBAND.

WELL, I THINK IT'S WONDERFUL THAT YOU'RE LOOKING AFTER YOUR OWN WELL-BEING.

I JUST WISH THE SCHOOL WASN'T SO FAR AWAY UP NORTH.

YEAH...

GIRLS, GET THESE DISHES CLEANED UP!

75

LATER, WHEN I CAME OUT AS A LESBIAN TO MY FAMILY, MY DAD UNLOADED THE BIG FAMILY SECRET:

YOU KNOW YOUR UNCLE DIED OF *AIDS*, RIGHT?

TUCKER!

NEAR THE END, HE MOVED IN WITH HIS PARENTS. HIS WAS THE FIRST RECORDED CASE OF *HIV* AT THEIR SOUTHERN SMALL-TOWN HOSPITAL.

I WISH HE'D STAYED IN THE CITY. AT LEAST THE DOCTORS THERE HAD *SOME* EXPERIENCE TREATING *HIV*.

BUT IN 1986 IT WAS A DEATH SENTENCE, NO MATTER WHAT.

I USED TO DATE WOMEN EXCLUSIVELY...

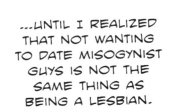

...UNTIL I REALIZED THAT NOT WANTING TO DATE MISOGYNIST GUYS IS NOT THE SAME THING AS BEING A LESBIAN.

THE MALE-BODIED PEOPLE I DO HOOK UP WITH ARE USUALLY GENDERQUEER, AND ARE *ALWAYS* POSSESSED OF A HUGE, THROBBING BRAIN.

EXTREMELY GEEKY AND CLEVER SHIRT

MY GIRLFRIEND IS ALSO POLY, WHICH IS GOOD, SINCE I'M IN A 24/7 RELATIONSHIP WITH MY DISSERTATION.

FOR THE MOST PART, I DO APPRECIATE THAT MY GIRLFRIEND DOESN'T MAKE ME LOOK STRAIGHT.

FAG

FAG

FAG

AFTER ALL, I WASN'T LOOKING TO TRANSITION SOCIALLY.

I DIDN'T START *T* UNTIL I FELT I'D EXHAUSTED ALL OTHER OPTIONS FOR GETTING MY MIND AND BODY INTO ALIGNMENT.

AND I STILL HAVE ETHICAL CONCERNS ABOUT PASSING AS A GUY IN A SYSTEM WHERE THIS CONFERS PRIVILEGES I DIDN'T EARN.

SO, HYPATIA OF ALEXANDRIA.

SINCE I KNOW YOU ALL DID THE READING, YOU CAN TELL ME THE SALACIOUS DETAILS OF HOW SHE DIED.

80

I DON'T WANT TO MAKE BEING CALLED FEMALE AN INSULT.

PLUS, IT CAN BE A FUN EDUCATIONAL TOOL.

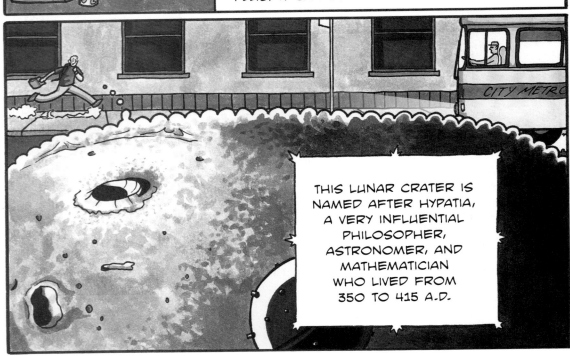

THIS LUNAR CRATER IS NAMED AFTER HYPATIA, A VERY INFLUENTIAL PHILOSOPHER, ASTRONOMER, AND MATHEMATICIAN WHO LIVED FROM 350 TO 415 A.D.

SHE WAS A TEACHER AT THE GREEK SCHOOL IN ALEXANDRIA IN EGYPT.

SAILORS USED HER NAVIGATION CHARTS FOR OVER A THOUSAND YEARS.

I DON'T REALLY EXPECT TO LEAD THE WAY TO TRUE SOCIAL JUSTICE...

BUT I DON'T MIND HELPING NAVIGATE.

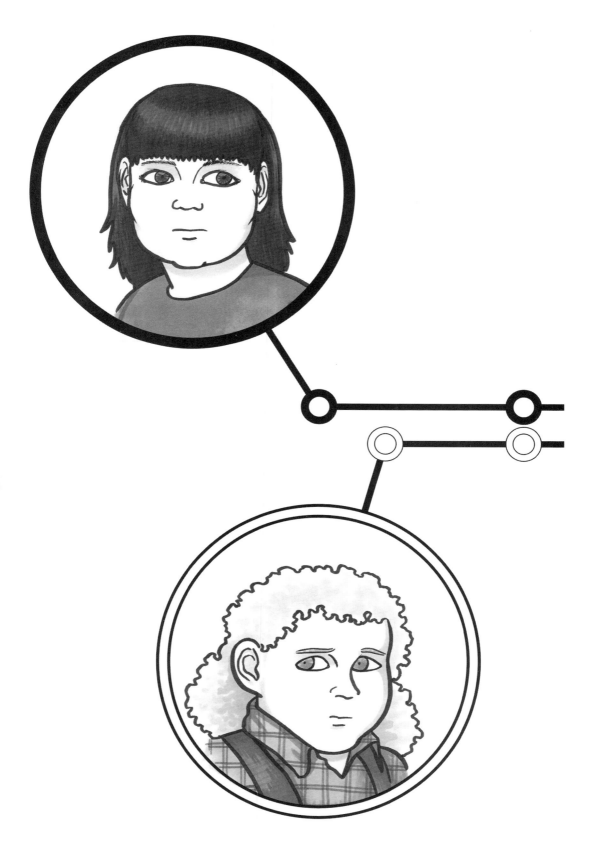

I WAS THEN CAST IN THE LEAD ROLE FOR MY DRAMA CLASS PRODUCTION.

THE CHARACTER WAS "ANYBODY," A SCREWUP WITH A GOOD HEART. I PLAYED HIM AS A BOY.

I HARBORED A FANTASY OF PLAYING LITTLE ORPHAN ANNIE ON BROADWAY, DESPITE NOT LOOKING ANYTHING LIKE HER.

A BOTTLE OF HAIR DYE, A PERM, AND COLORED CONTACTS WOULD BRIDGE THE GAP BETWEEN US.

WHEN I WAS 13 MY MOTHER REMARRIED. THIS ONE HAD A HAIR FETISH.

ONCE I FIGURED OUT HE'D LEAVE ME ALONE IF I CUT MY HAIR, I KEPT IT SHORT UNTIL I WENT AWAY TO COLLEGE.

I STARTED HIGH SCHOOL AT 13.

I HAD CRUSHES ON BOTH GIRLS AND BOYS, BUT DIDN'T EXPECT THE GIRLS TO RECIPROCATE, SO I JUST DATED THE BOYS.

I DIDN'T DATE IN HIGH SCHOOL.

SIGH

SIGH

I HAD HORRIBLE, UNREQUITED CRUSHES ON STRANGE, UGLY BOYS WHO HAD HORRIBLE, UNREQUITED CRUSHES ON GOOD-LOOKING GIRLS.

I FOUND A NICE, SAFE BOY MY JUNIOR YEAR OF HIGH SCHOOL.

WE BECAME INSEPARABLE, ENJOYED AN ENTHUSIASTIC SEX LIFE, AND GOT ENGAGED.

A YEAR INTO COMMUNITY COLLEGE I TURNED 18, AND WE MARRIED.

NOT TOO LONG AFTER THAT I FOUND OUT I WAS PREGNANT.

WHEN IT CAME TIME FOR COLLEGE, I CHOSE BRYN MAWR BECAUSE I THOUGHT THE CAMPUS WAS GORGEOUS.

I HAD TERRIBLE PTSD, NO STUDY SKILLS, AND WAS ABOUT TO LEAP INTO AN ELITE WOMEN'S COLLEGE IN MAINLINE PHILADELPHIA.

IN OTHER WORDS, I HAD NO IDEA WHAT I WAS GETTING INTO.

I'D ALWAYS ASSUMED I'D GET A DEGREE AND BECOME SOME SORT OF WHITE-COLLAR PROFESSIONAL.

INSTEAD, I WAS 20 AND MARRIED WITH A BABY...

GETTING WELFARE BENEFITS...

AND WORKING IN LOW-WAGE, DEAD-END JOBS.

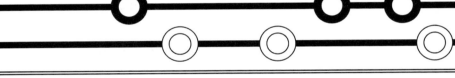

ONE DAY MY FRIEND JOAN, A 6-FOOT-TALL LACROSSE PLAYER, ASKED ME FOR A BACKRUB AND STARTED TO REMOVE LAYERS OF CLOTHING.

I PANICKED AND FLED.

IT HAD NEVER OCCURRED TO ME TO HAVE SEX WITH A WOMAN.

PREGNANCY HAD FORCED ME TO FOCUS ON MY BODY, AND IT FELT BAD.

I COULDN'T STAND TO BE TOUCHED.

MY HUSBAND AND I BECAME PHYSICALLY DISTANT, AND I WAS SLIDING INTO DEPRESSION.

I TOLD A FRIEND ABOUT THE INCIDENT AND SHE WAS THRILLED.

THRILLED?

WHY, WE'VE ALL BEEN WAITING FOR YOU TO COME OUT!

...

YOU THINK I'M A LESBIAN?

OF COURSE YOU'RE A DYKE! WHY DO YOU THINK YOU'RE SO MASCULINE?

I WENT BACK TO SCHOOL FOR TECHNICAL WRITING. AFTER MY FIRST SEMESTER, MY HUSBAND AND I DIVORCED AMICABLY.

DEPRESSION MADE IT IMPOSSIBLE TO COPE WITH SCHOOL AND SINGLE MOTHERHOOD, SO HE TOOK CUSTODY OF OUR SON.

I BEGAN TO HAUNT GAY BARS BY MYSELF TO SEE IF THAT WAS THE LIFE I WAS LOOKING FOR.

OBLIGATORY VEST

AS MUCH AS I WANTED TO SLEEP WITH MEN I WASN'T HAVING ANY LUCK (ESPECIALLY SINCE I KEPT GETTING CRUSHES ON GAY GUYS).

SO I DECIDED MAYBE MY FRIENDS HAD A POINT.

I HAD SERIOUS DOUBTS ABOUT THIS NEW IDENTITY, BUT HEY, IT MEANT I MIGHT ACTUALLY GET LAID FOR A CHANGE.

I EVENTUALLY HOOKED UP WITH A GIRL I MET AT THE BAR.

THE SEX WAS STRANGE

AND FAMILIAR

AND GENTLE.

SHE STILL LIVED WITH HER EX. BEING ALLERGIC TO DRAMA AND UNAWARE THAT THIS WAS A COMMON ARRANGEMENT AMONGST LESBIANS, I DROVE HER HOME AND THAT WAS THAT.

I EVENTUALLY HOOKED UP WITH LANA.

SOMETIMES SHE LOOKED LIKE A MAN, AND IT FIT.

THEN SOMETHING WOULD CHANGE AND SHE'D LOOK LIKE A WOMAN, AND I'D FEEL INEXPLICABLY SAD.

AT SCHOOL, I STARTED SKIPPING THE LAST HOUR OF MY THURSDAY CLASS SO I COULD ATTEND THE LGBT STUDENT MEETINGS.

I MAINLY MADE FRIENDS WITH THE GUYS.

I COULDN'T FIGURE OUT WHY I DIDN'T FIT IN WITH THE LESBIANS.

I HAD ASSUMED THEY'D BE MORE BUTCH, BUT THE WOMEN I MET WERE FEMININE.

MY CRAPPY STUDY SKILLS CAUGHT UP WITH ME, AND I FLUNKED OUT MY SOPHOMORE YEAR.

I HEADED BACK TO THE MIDWEST, DETERMINED TO FIND THE RADICAL FEMINIST LESBIANS THERE.

I WAS WORKING MY FIRST TECH WRITING JOB AFTER COLLEGE.

I LIKED MY COWORKERS AND MY BOSS, BUT I WAS SLIDING INTO DEPRESSION AGAIN.

I KEPT CALLING IN TO WORK.

I'D SIT IN THE DARKENED APARTMENT, CHAIN-SMOKING AND READING MY GAY ROOMMATE'S BOOKS ABOUT GENDER PERFORMANCE.

INSTEAD, I FOUND SAM. SHE WAS NOT VERY RADICAL, OR A FEMINIST, AND I CAN'T EVEN REMEMBER IF SHE IDENTIFIED AS A LESBIAN.

BUT SHE LOOKED LIKE A GUY AND WOULD RATHER LOSE A CRAPPY JOB THAN WEAR THE WOMEN'S UNIFORM.

WELCOME TO LOU'S PANCAKE HOUSE

PLEASE WAIT to be SEATED

MY BOSS SAID THIS COULDN'T CONTINUE, THAT I HAD TO DO SOMETHING.

SO I WENT TO A PSYCHIATRIST AND STARTED TAKING ANTI-DEPRESSANTS, WHICH GAVE ME THE EMOTIONAL STRENGTH TO GET BACK ON TRACK.

MEANWHILE, I WAS READING *STONE BUTCH BLUES.*

I DIDN'T IDENTIFY WITH FEINBERG'S CHARACTER PER SE, BUT THE STORY STILL SHOWED ME A POSSIBILITY I HADN'T SERIOUSLY CONSIDERED BEFORE.

AND SO IT WENT: I'D FALL FOR EVERY PROTO-TRANSMAN I'D MEET.

BUT I DIDN'T KNOW TRANSMEN EXISTED, SO TO ME IT LOOKED LIKE I MUST BE A DYKE.

AND THAT IDENTITY MADE SENSE TO EVERYONE ELSE: I WAS A DYKE.

NOT A LESBIAN, NOT BI.

JUST A DYKE.

I BEGAN RESEARCHING FTMs ONLINE. A COPY OF LOREN CAMERON'S *BODY ALCHEMY* MADE ME REALIZE THERE WAS A GENUINE OPPORTUNITY HERE.

I HIT THE GYM TO SEE HOW I MIGHT START TO CHANGE MY BODY TO MATCH MY DESIRES.

NOT LONG AFTER, I CAME OUT AS TRANS.

I EVENTUALLY MADE MY WAY BACK TO THE NORTHEAST, AND SETTLED INTO A SEXLESS RELATIONSHIP WITH YET ANOTHER AMBIGUOUSLY-GENDERED LESBIAN.

I WENT BACK TO SCHOOL FOR PROGRAMMING, THE INTERNET BUBBLE PICKED ME UP, AND OFF I WENT AS A CONSULTANT.

AFTER I STARTED T, I CONTINUED TO DATE BOTH MEN AND WOMEN, INCLUDING THIS ONE BUTCH DYKE I MET ONLINE.

WE LIVED IN DIFFERENT STATES, BUT WOULD HOOK UP WHEN WE'D TRAVEL NEAR EACH OTHER.

FIVE YEARS LATER THE TECH BUBBLE BURSTS...

MY RELATIONSHIP COLLAPSES UNDER ITS OWN WEIGHT...

AND I'M LEFT PROFESSIONALLY AND EMOTIONALLY ADRIFT.

DANA AND I DIDN'T KEEP DATING, BUT WE HAD BECOME VERY GOOD FRIENDS AND KEPT IN TOUCH.

I MADE PLANS TO VISIT.

SHE'D TOLD ME ABOUT A NEW GIRLFRIEND, WHOM I WAS KEEN TO MEET.

I WENT TO A GENDER-THEMED POETRY SLAM, JUST FOR SOMETHING TO DO, AND STARTED DATING A BUTCH GIRL I MET THERE. WE EVENTUALLY MOVED IN TOGETHER.

ONE EVENING, A FRIEND OF HERS FROM OUT OF TOWN VISITED. HE WAS MAYBE THE FIRST TRANS GUY I'D TALKED TO.

LONG AFTER DANA WENT TO BED, HE AND I STAYED UP TALKING ABOUT TRANS STUFF.

DANA AND I SPLIT UP RIGHT AFTER I CAME OUT. WE STAYED FRIENDS, BUT I NEEDED TO FIND OUT WHO MY PEOPLE WERE.

JAMES AND I MADE PLANS TO MEET UP AT THE CONFERENCE.

SINCE HE WAS NEW TO THE QUEER TRANSGUY SCENE, I WAS GOING TO SHOW HIM AROUND.

BE KIND OF A BIG BROTHER.

I STARTED FOLLOWING AARON WITHOUT REALLY THINKING OF WHAT I WAS GOING TO DO IF I CAUGHT HIM.

THEN IT SNOWED AND WE WERE STUCK THERE SUNDAY NIGHT.

WE COULD HANG OUT AT THE HOTEL BAR, I GUESS.

...MY SON?

WE'RE BACK IN TOUCH, ACTUALLY.

HE WAS ANGRY FOR AWHILE, LIKE MY TRANSITION WAS SOMETHING I DID TO PUNISH HIM.

BUT NOW HE ACCEPTS THINGS AS THEY ARE. JUST NEEDED TIME TO COME AROUND ON HIS OWN.

SO, HOW ABOUT YOU?

I.... UH... HEARD ABOUT YOU AND DANA.

YEAH...

IT'S HARD TO HAVE SPENT SO MUCH ENERGY ON AN IDENTITY THAT FIT SO BADLY.

AND TO HAVE LOST THAT FEELING OF HAVING A FAMILY.

IF THIS TRANS THING DOESN'T FIT, WHERE WILL I GO? WHO THE HELL AM I?

THE NEXT DAY AARON TRIED TO ACT NONCHALANT.

AFTER THAT FAILED, IT WAS CLEAR WE WERE SMITTEN.

I KNEW JAMES WAS A REAL GEM BECAUSE HE ALWAYS TOLD ME EVERYTHING.

HE HAS THE SAME FETISH ABOUT HONESTY THAT I DO.

WE DID THE LONG-DISTANCE THING FOR SEVERAL MONTHS, BUT IT QUICKLY BECAME CLEAR THAT WE NEEDED TO BE IN THE SAME PLACE.

WE HAD A COMPLETELY DO-IT-YOURSELF WEDDING.

WE COOKED EVERYTHING, AND JAMES SEWED OUR WEDDING GARB AND ALL THE DECORATIONS.

THE WEDDING ITSELF WAS A WARM BLUR. IT TRULY FELT LIKE THE CELEBRATION WE WANTED.

WE ALSO KNOW WE CAN THROW ONE HELL OF A PARTY TOGETHER.

HONESTLY? I NEVER THOUGHT I'D WANT
TO GET MARRIED, BUT I LIKE IT.

WE ARE FULLY
DOMESTIC AND
VERY HAPPY TO BE
DOMESTICATED.

TALKING ABOUT HOW WE HAVE MADE
OUR FAMILY FOR OURSELVES BRINGS
JAMES TO HAPPY TEARS.

WE ARE TRULY CONTENT.

EPILOGUE

CAL CONTINUES TO EXPLORE VARIOUS ASPECTS OF KINKDOM, AND HAS DONE SO WITH CIS GAY MEN, QUEER TRANSMEN, AND EVEN THE OCCASIONAL GENDERQUEER DYKE. HE NOW LIVES WITH HIS LONG-TERM QFTM PARTNER, AND ENJOYS A PRETTY NORMAL LIFE OF WORK, OUTDOORS ACTIVITIES, AND, OF COURSE, KINKY SEX.

HENRY'S REAL NAME IS MARTY, AND HE DOESN'T CARE WHO KNOWS IT. HE POSTS PROFLIGATE SMUT ALL OVER THE INTERNET AS TERATOMARTY. HE DOES NOT ACTUALLY LIVE IN A MUSEUM DEDICATED TO THE MINUTIAE OF HIS LIFE, BUT HE WOULD IF HE COULD. THAT, OR A HAUNTED CASTLE.

SHORTLY AFTER HIS BREAKUP WITH MARNI, ADAM TRANSITIONED AND BEGAN LIVING FULL-TIME AS A GAY MAN. A COUPLE OF YEARS LATER HE MET JUSTIN, A CIS GAY MAN, AND THE TWO HAVE BEEN TOGETHER FIFTEEN YEARS AND COUNTING.

BLAKE MANAGES HIS HEALTH WITH THE HELP OF HIS PROVIDER. HE HAS COME TO REALIZE THAT DISCLOSURE CAN BE SEXY AND FUN RATHER THAN A HINDRANCE TO HOOKING UP. IN FACT, WHEN HE CAN BE COMPLETELY NAKED WITH HIS PARTNERS, SAFE SEX IS EVEN MORE PLEASURABLE.

AVERY IS TOO BUSY FINISHING HIS DISSERTATION TO WRITE A BIO. SINCE THIS STORY WAS WRITTEN, HE HAS RECEIVED NUMEROUS FELLOWSHIPS AND RESEARCH GRANTS FOR HIS SCHOLARLY WORK.

AARON AND JAMES CONTINUE TO LIVE IN DOMESTIC BLISS. JAMES IS HAPPILY EMPLOYED AS A PROGRAMMER, AND AARON IS A MAGAZINE EDITOR AND WRITER. DANA REMAINS A CLOSE FRIEND OF THEIRS TO THIS DAY, AND IS AN IMPORTANT PART OF THEIR CHOSEN FAMILY.

Acknowledgements

Thanks to Mom & Dad, Jeremy & Jodi, and the fam for general support. To Jeanne Thornton, Toren K. Smith, and Carrie & Eric for reading and commenting. To Alison Bechdel for recommending me for this project initially. To all the many friends who have expressed their support and enthusiasm for this project.

Special thanks to Allison Trzop, Alex Kapitan, and Joanna Green. Your hard work unquestionably made this a better book.

Finally, a huge thanks to Cal, Henry, Adam, Blake, Avery, Aaron, and James for sharing their stories with me and for patiently slogging through multiple drafts.

About the Author

The cartoons of Dylan Edwards (the artist occasionally known as "NDR") have been published in a variety of venues, both in print and online, including the Fantagraphics anthology *No Straight Lines*.

You may remember him from such comics as his ongoing series *Politically InQueerect*, his sports-themed cartoon "The Outfield" (published on *OutSports.com* from 2002-2009), and an editorial cartoon focusing on queer issues that ran from 2004-2005 in the *Texas Triangle* and *TXT Newsmagazine*.

Transposes is his first full-length book.

You can read more of his comics at *studiondr.com*.